Stella Maidment

Illustrated by
Emiliano Miligrado
and Joelle Dreidemy

Welcome to the Garden

There's lots to see. Come and have a look!

Vegetables

Pets

Pond

Tree house

Flower bed

Bees

Ants

Lawn

Birds

This baby snail is hiding inside the book. Can you find him in every scene?

Can you spot
these things?

carrots   marrow   fork

green tomato   watering can

Ants are small but very strong. They work together to find food and build nests.

Cats and dogs are the most popular pets. Dogs sweat through their feet. Cats cannot sweat!

You can sometimes see dragonflies hovering over garden ponds. They lay their eggs in the water.

Can you spot these things?

woodlouse   grasshopper

crown   football   toy car

Can you spot these things?

spider's web   white rabbit   toadstool   green apple   logs

Squirrels build their homes in trees using twigs and moss. A squirrel's nest is called a drey.

How many squirrels can you count?

Bees do a special dance to tell each other where the best flowers are.

Birds sing different songs to attract a mate, warn of danger or guard their nest.

Can you spot these things?   chicken   basket   toy plane   red flowers   nesting box

Can you spot these things?

skipping rope

teddy bear

mouse

cat

bat

More to spot

Go back and find these scenes in the book!

Did you find me?

Did you Know?

Grasshoppers and crickets are great at jumping. Some can jump 50 times the length of their body in one big leap.

A butterfly's bright colours aren't just for decoration. They warn birds that the butterfly might be poisonous.

Some ants' nests have lots of different rooms. They even have a room for their rubbish!

Snails can't hear but they can see and they are very good at smelling.

The name 'centipede' means 'a hundred feet'. Most centipedes have between 30 and 50, but that's still a lot of feet!

More garden fun!

Minibeast hotel

Make a pile of sticks and stones in a dark, quiet corner of your garden or a local park. Wait a few days and then go and look carefully inside. Your hotel should already have some special little guests!

Hide and seek

Choose a cuddly toy that you can hide around your home or garden for a friend or family member to spot, just like the snail in the book! You could hide other objects and make a list of things to find.

Popcorn for birds

Ask an adult to help you make some plain popcorn without any sugar or salt. Thread the popcorn on to some string or a thin ribbon using a large, blunt needle. Hang the chain outside for the birds to eat.

Fun butterfly poster

Draw butterfly outlines on pieces of paper. Ask your friends and family to add patterns and colours using crayons or pens. Cut out the butterflies and stick them on a big sheet of paper to make a poster.

Designer: Krina Patel
Editor: Tasha Percy
Editorial Director: Victoria Garrard
Art Director: Laura Roberts-Jensen

Copyright © QED Publishing 2014

First published in the UK in 2014 by
QED Publishing
A Quarto Group company
The Old Brewery,
6 Blundell Street,
London, N7 9BH

www.qed-publishing.co.uk

A catalogue record for this book is available from the British Library.

ISBN 978 1 78171 656 4

Printed in China